CW00544871

The Black Dog's Day

Patrick Gordon-Duff-Pennington

with original drawings by
Alasdair McMorrine

Hayloft Publishing Ltd
Cumbria

First published 2017 by Hayloft Publishing Ltd.

A CIP catalogue record for this book is available from the British Library

ISBN 978-1-910237-26-7

Designed, printed and bound in the EU

Hayloft policy is to use papers that are natural, renewable and re-cyclable products and made from wood grown in sustainable forests. The logging and manufacturing processes are expected to conform to the environmental regulations of the country of origin.

Hayloft Publishing Ltd,
a company registered in England number 4802586
2 Staveley Mill Yard, Staveley, Kendal, LA8 9LR (registered office)
L'Ancien Presbytère, 21460 Corsaint, France (editorial office)

Email: books@hayloft.eu
Tel: 07971 352473

www.hayloft.eu

Dedication

The dedication of this book is a long litany of thanks to Canon James Baker – a fellow revolutionary, his wife Anne lately Vicar of Muncaster and the Churches of Eskdale, and Alison Newcome, long suffering spouse of the Bishop of Carlisle.

For my parents, my teachers and family and for the people who have loved me and cared for me and taught me through all of my 86 years; for those who have led me in my blindness to wonderful places in hills and islands which most people are never lucky enough to see. They taught me to speak out without fear on behalf of those less privileged than me. Many of them had so little but took me into their homes and gave so much. To Hector Monro, Alick Buchanan–Smith, Russell Johnston and George Younger who fought so hard on behalf of common sense against philosophies of a theocratic government in the 1980s and 90s. For John McFall who came to me as a student from the Industry and Parliament Trust and became Chairman of the Treasury Select Committee. For Kenneth Mackenzie, Sam Mitha, and so many others in the Civil Service who became my friends and taught me discretion – if not respect – in dealing with the guardians of the public morals, even though the ethics of their posts gagged them.

Thanks are also due to Eric Robson who published my first two books, Isabel Fraser of the BBC, and

Fordyce Maxwell of the 'Scotsman'. To Jo Wagstaff and Sarah Knowles who translated my illegible writing into a legible text and above all to Dawn Robertson of Hayloft Publishing who published these poems at a time when it is very difficult to find a publisher to produce the work of a little known writer. Finally to Alasdair McMorrine my friend, who made the illustrations and the drawing for the cover.

Patrick of the Hills, 2016

CONTENTS

A Firm Truth – Rediscovery

'Oh! Who were you?' they said.
How could they ask so stupidly
When you are written in my eyes?
Before you came
Life had but little point,
Rising and falling like an endless sea
In monotones.
I rose at six, and worked all day,
Asleep by half past ten at night;
I watched the dawn drift wearily through
window panes;
I did the office work,
And spoke to tourists in the afternoon;
I dined off silver plates
With rich Americans.
Drank wine at dinner time
And walked the woods and fields without an aim.

But then you came
And all those little pointless chores
Gained new significance.
I heard and saw once more –
A blackbird's song, a falling autumn leaf;
A flap of startled pigeons' wings;
And rooks going home to roost at night
As winds begin to rustle through the distant trees.

continues...

Before you came,
Almost it was as though my heart was deaf,
But now, for you, too late I know, but still
I'll turn the silver in my pocket when the moon is new,
And find once more my childhood innocence.

Robin McCall – In Memoriam

I'm very much upset at this man dying –
He was so much a part of my life
And the life of all those who loved him
That even the thought of him no longer there
Is a weight on our will to live.
I see him still – the way he always was
When first we met and he taught me there
How to survive in a hostile world
Where the snow, drifted by the wind,
Mounted up the windows, and we shovelled for days
And days to reach the road –
When the porridge simmered all night
For our breakfast and he and I
Would sit by the fire at Ruskich
Of an evening, both of us sound asleep
In our chairs while Peggie sat between us
Doing her mending or darning our socks,
He taught me – eventually – how to back a tractor;
How to strain a fence;
How to sow fertiliser out of a sheet;
How to cut the logs and set the snares
For the endless rabbits who made their runs
Through the fences below the woods which were
filled
With primroses and violets in spring.
He taught me how to milk a cow
Or lamb a ewe – after a fashion.
He taught me – terrifying ignorance –
How to inject a lamb and dose a tup.

Above all he taught me how to swing
With the world as we climbed the hill
On our way to the gathering in the early morning;
And a thousand other things did this man teach me.
I know that his family
Will feel a gaping hole in their everyday lives
And that I, like them, must learn
To still breathe fire,
The world turns yet and now, because of him
And the wisdom that he taught to those whose life he
touched,
It is we who must learn to survive
In the places he taught us to love.

Muriel Hall – In Memoriam

Lovely woman, lasting friend
This is only a note of our distant sympathy
For David, and Jo, and all of your family
Only to let you know we'll never forget you
Wherever you've gone –
You in the yard, being pulled down the drive
By grandchildren and their fairly unruly dogs.
You at the playground, you in the yard,
You at the office, always you
With those eyes and memorable smile
Which lit up the lives of all who you met,
You washed up, handing the drinks
To innumerable guests in the old Great Hall
At dinners and weddings,
You probably seething inside
But never cross – that's how it seemed.
You brought all of your goodness to
Our home, and now, just know
That your memory will always survive
As the wonderful lady who lit up our days.
Thank you for being such a gift in our family's lives.
You'll always be here, still close watching over us,
Still part of our everyday too.
Be happy wherever you've gone
And because of you, we'll try, in the sadness of now,
To remember a lady, and teach ourselves to smile
once more.
That's how much you meant – and mean – to all of us.

Beyond Creag Uanach
AECM

For Dougie Langlands – On his retirement

I remember you
As tutor to my ignorance
For all but forty years
And see you still, in my mind's eye,
A distant memory
Of that small child at school
Who Margaret Payne had told me was
A quite delightful little boy
Roaming Lochinver's playground at the school
Those countless moons ago;
And I remember
Your first season at Ardverikie
Roaming with you across the perpendicular slopes
In May to shoot a stag
Which ran as fast as us.
You held me by my ankles
To get a shot at the poor beast below
And afterwards I can still see
The scarlet cloudberries in a hollow
At the bottom of the hill.
I see you still
As tutor to my children
In the ways of deer or teaching them
To cast a fly, or shoot, and later still
To my grandchildren.
I hear your words
Philosopher among the Highland hills,
Thinking your revolutionary thoughts
And sometimes stating them quite hard

Which might have shocked our London based
associates
Who thought that Scotland was no more
Than just a place to kill a stag
Or shoot a grouse.
And now, I see you crouched,
Among those precious places which
I have loved for all my eighty years
As part of Them, as part of the deer
That you have lived with for such a long time now,
Learning to outsmart them in the wayward wind,
Cultivating a patience that your mother
Never knew you had.

I see you on the top of Beinn a' Chlachair
With the ptarmigan running in front of you
Among the stones or watching the eagle's flight,
Or gralloching a stag at the King's Well,
Or at the shooting of the foxes.
I see you, crawling like a snake
To stalk a stag, the clients burn behind you
On the skyline, all too visible to watching deer.

And now, one final time
It's I who see you in my mind
Leading down the path at dusk, with you
And the pony and the stag's horn
Etched against the moonlit sky
Returning home for one last time
At evening.

You've more than earned your rest.

In Cages

I know
How animals in cages feel,
For not so long ago
I walked the mountain tops
And felt my legs swing free across the summer grass,
But now I'm here
Imprisoned in a gilded cage by circumstance.
I've lost my freedom, lost my hope,
And never more may know
The sun upon my moving limbs,
The music of the wind among the rocks;
So now I understand how lions feel
In cages.

Dreams of Stillness

You are the pool of stillness
That I seek so desperately
To discipline the wildness
Of my daily life
With all the hither and thither
Of its frantic swinging
To and fro
From North to South,
To East to West.
I have no peace,
Seeking for something that I know,
Deep in my heart,
I'm destined not to find.
So when at night
Before I sleep
I find your gentleness
Tingeing my thoughts,
It is with gratitude
I recognise your stillness
As the drug I need so much
To calm the fury of my hectic life
And let me dream.

An Early Autumn

Beloved,
You sleep tonight outside my arms,
The days troop sadly by
With you not here,
Their dull recession broken only
By the violent storms.
The land is tired this week,
The trees lie down to die,
And golden medallions fill the stormy days,
Where leaves give up their late pretence
Of summer dance
And wander aimlessly about the autumn sky.

I met a robin in the hall today,
The greylags seek the sheltered pools,
While in the wind tossed woods
The fallen trees,
Roots weakened by the summer drought,
Release their hold upon the sodden soil.
It is a time of tears,
With ancient friends cast motionless upon the ground.

I ask myself, ‘Will spring return,
Will you?’
This week it rained
As though the Gods were cross,
But when you called
The sun came out
And all the world was pacified again.

Adam and Eve

Remember all the talk we had
Of apple trees last year,
And picking apples after harvest time?
This week
The spring has come again
And quickening of blood
As blossom petals drift
Across the Maytime wind.
We ask ourselves once more,
After the grain is gathered in
Under some golden moon
Will apples ever be
Ripe red enough to pick again,
Or will the apple season
Never come?

BUTTERFLIES NEED A GARDEN

Yesterday in the afternoon
I watched the butterflies flitting along their flight path
Among the brambles by the riverside.
Like them and the swallows
I know that we need somewhere of our own
As a place to which to return, year in, year out.
Let it be soon
We find a house
Where we can go to rest
Without the malaise of the separate roofs at night
And agony of living out
Our semi-separate lives
For months on end, apart.
For many years
We've known deep down inside ourselves
The course our lives should take.
Since then we've learned each other's ways.
Sometimes I've tried to make myself annoyed
At little things you do or say
Which might have made me hopping mad.
I've tried to match you limb for limb
Asleep enfolded in your arms at night.
Thinking how things could be,
I sometimes tell myself
If you did this or that
Such time as we have struck the barrel hoops
That bind our present state.
I might be hurt, or sad, or cross,
But now instead I always end up laughing
So I never quite succeed.

Goodnight, my Sweet!

Goodnight, my sweet!
I'll close the shutters on the windows now.
For one short sharp triumphant week
I let your sunshine stream across my life.

I watched the foxes in the hollow on the rocks
Above the hawthorn tree on Bessiewalla Hill,
Stalking the rabbits at the fringes of the whins,
I carted stones, and sowed the grass
Under the twisting peewit's wings.

And when I climbed the hill again
I sang old songs for you.
Trailing my toes among the meadow flowers
Higher and higher, till I crossed the drain
Where the forget-me-nots still grow.

I moved the cattle, dosed the sheep;
Sent eighty two fat lambs, away
And jagged the pet lambs for pulpy kidney once again
All this I did with you in mind,
But now I know it's time to say
Goodnight, my sweet!

Two times this week I left at five,
And wasn't back until the middle of the night
I took your memory along the dawning roads.
Once to the North, away into the morning hills,
I passed quite close, and guessed your sleeping head;

Had tea and toast with John Forbes at Killiecrankie
While half the world was still at rest,
And cows unconscious in the soaking fields.
The wide grey ribbon of the hissing road
Stretched endlessly until I came
Within sight of the Grey Mountains
Where all the rivers rise which tumble down to home
Where I was nurtured near the edge of Findhorn Bay.

Always, always, my sweet,
That sight means home to me,
With the Catlodge sycamore tree,
And the Spey winding through the Laggan fields.
And just this week I stole the thought of you,
And took the warmth of you
Among the families for whom I fight.
I feel so alone in the fight sometimes,
Can you understand?

Can you understand?
When the men who don't need help
Stand sneering in the market place
And talk only about 'the viable units',
And all the, 'idle hopeless Highlanders',
I tell you all of this because, for a while,
I felt my courage falter, and my strength gone,
But then I sat beside you once,
Writing back to front in the room at Connachan
When Roy Mackenzie Charrington was there,
And now I'm strong again.
But now, my sweet, it's time to say goodnight!

Armed with the knowledge of you
I called in on Kenneth and Margaret Mackay.
He is a famous piping judge, and once a missionary
in Bolivia.
He set up the first mission hospital in the jungle
Before he married Margaret
Who came from a croft opposite the Summer Isles.
They've gone, those days, when the men danced
The Irish jig on the boards at the Games,
But I remember the fluttering of the Balmoral ribbons
On the back of my neck in the June wind.

I called on Kat Pelham-Burn too,
She got stuck in the flat with my mother
In my grandfather's house before Vera and I were born
Vera's in jail now, and when she's not there
She's in the bar, or else underneath the arches.
I don't suppose she's any worse than I,
Harbouring all the strength of loving you illicitly,
Letting the warmth of you smiling,
Rush me along the road, where I often travel in the
winter
Under the sweeping curtain of the Northern Lights.
But yes, I know, it's time to say goodnight, my sweet!

I sat on the tailboard of the car parked
Outside the shop at Laggan bridge
And talked to all the world.
Ian MacGillivray unshaved, Davie Millar,
Joan Richardson, the doctor's wife,
Dying and lost her faith,
Wondering what I had found, and she had not,
A sad wreck of a woman, once intelligent.

Reflections, Loch Laggan
AECM

I could have told her what it was I'd found
Through you. The way of seeing simple things,
Of feeling warm, of saying what I think,
But you know it perfectly well,
And when you're next on top of the hill with Spy,
Look down towards night at the blue and silent night
To the west beyond Ibert,
And you will realise, just as well as I
That some values can never change.
This is what you gave me in a week, not knowing,
But now, my love, it's time to say goodnight!

Hughie Milne, I saw too,
In the house beyond the old school,
The seas of Ardnamurchan still breaking in piercing
eyes
Of eighty years away,
Driven to deafness by a talking wife

John Duncan is my oldest friend,
Stalker, and ally, and teacher of the hills of boyhood.
We used to worm our way right into the middle
Of huge herds of September stags.
Breathless with excitement among the deer
On the plateau by the Coignafeam march.
When I was in the army, sometimes I would stay
In the spotless house, and washed in the cold water
In the basin on the pinewood table
At dawn, before walking across the
Down to Fort Augustus, among the sweetbriars
Above Cullachy woods.
At night it used to be very quiet,
And now, with you about to be shut out,
It's very quiet once more.

Communications – L.M.A.

Sometimes,
Watching the sky outside the window
When you're not there,
I sit here at your desk
Wishing you were
To put a hand upon my shoulder
To calm me down.
Other people
Know nothing of my life elsewhere –
To struggle with the politicians and the authorities
To gain a better life for country people,
Not merely
To preserve the status quo,
But to establish
Some sound framework for their future welfare –
And yet you know
The weekly travelling and reaching back
To the security of this,
The one safe place I know
Have taken toll,
Until at last I have no expectations left –
Only the thought of your communicating hand
Upon my shoulder,
As I sometimes sit at your desk
When you're not there.

Caring and Happiness

When the sun has scorched me,
You are the cooling waters and my shading trees;
When the snow has chilled me,
You, the warmth of my fire and my peats glow;
When I am sad or lonely,
You, the blue mountains that lift my heart,
And when I stray,
Ever it is your caring eyes
Which give the strength and happiness
To guide me home.

An Endless Road

I sat in the chair this morning quite relaxed
In the corner of my dressing room
Face to face with Death
'You come with me' the lady said
And thus it crossed my mind
How simple it might be
To slip away in quiet oblivion
Manacled to her, but life
Is not so easy and I had to stay
Pulling on my socks, wondering what
The point of living still might be,
Lingering on an endless road
To God knows where,
Oft terrorised by endless pain
And knowing all too well
It's still a long hard furrow that I have to plough
To reach my resting place and home
Beyond this tiresome day

Poppies in the Fields Again
(Between East Linton and Haddington)

What could this beauty mean –
This sunrise on East Lothian countryside;
The roses twining among the hawthorn hedge,
And fields of grain
Coming to harvest time again.
If you were not
The one for whom my life was meant
Entwined with me
The way the briars
In hedges twine
In summer time

What point would be to life
Without you now?
What could this beauty be –
No sweetness felt
Without you always there to share.
To share the summer sight
Of day and night;
To notice scarlet poppies coming back
To grain fields underneath
The Moorfoot Hills
At harvest time?

Without you always there
To share my thoughts
And visions of the world
What could my Scotland mean?

Two Days in Provence

Warmth of reflected light
From ochre hills of Roussillon
And siskin flitting yellow green
Among the needles of the pines.
Views from the tops of the hills
On sunlit afternoons,
With memories of days
Well spent in company.
Internal turbulence of sleep-filled hours
With endless nightmares laced
With aftermath of chanterelles
After consuming too much food.
Papal palace in morning sun
At Avignon.
Goats at Oppede le Vieux
Cool of the château winery
Gouged from the rocks of Romanin.
Limestone hills and lunch at St Remy,
Lavender fields at Luberon.
The olive press at Mausanne-les-Alpilles
Van Gogh's asylum, Daudet's Mill
At Fontvielle.
Time so freely spent and given
These are my happy memories
Of winter in Provence.

The Shelter Stone

You found us there –
Two wild geese at the Shelter Stone,
And took us in;
Two thinkers free as eagles in the sky,
Free of each other's flight, yet tied
With bonds of need too strong to break.
You sheltered us
With kindness through those summer nights
Until our strength returned to journey on
Through hours and hours of absence
From each other's touch
But sometime soon our wings one day
Will bring us back on autumn wings
Into the arms of you, our caring friend
Who found us first in need of care
What seems a month of moons ago,
Beside the Shelter Stone –
That you call home.

LES AMBASSADEURS

Waiting –
Only for you!
Outside, London lashed with rain and wind,
And my mind with memories of so many years.
Slight unease while you walk to the telephone,
Then the pianist in the bar
Suddenly playing Chopin –
Themes from the first concerto, I think.
The music sweeping over my gloom,
Rushing all the sadness away –
All the sadness of the two of us.
Longing for a life together
Which tonight seems further away than ever;
But the music, and the wind, and the rain
Absolved our problems, and suddenly
Life became –
Possible again!

All the same –
The lecturer was a prat!

Hawaii

Even along the wires
Your voice across the world
Was like a primrose bud
Emerging in the darkest wood
After the winter's frost.

DEEP DOWN

The knowledge of our plaited roots
Twined safely through each other's memories
Gives me some strange security
In times of stress. You understand?
Without you now,
Beside me through every minute of my most
untidy day,
I think they'd have to bury me
Before another equinox, but as it is
I hold you in the safety net
Of every thought I have
Until the time you walk again
Smiling before too long,
Across the threshold of our home.

Night Without You

Nothing I have,
No gifts to give.
I have no hope,
No home to offer you;
No place to which to come
As haven in the endless storm.

I wander like a lone seabird
Flying through the black arches of the night
Beyond the Hebrides,
Searching for his lost mate
Among the white-topped waves.

I search the emptiness,
Endlessly search
For you, my love, my absent love
Knowing you're there and needing me
As I need you,
In all the turbulence,
I cannot reach you now, caged but secure
In another world you'll have to learn to understand.

My life you have.
My love you have.
Your love I think
I have, but I,
Like the lone seabird,
In endless flight,
Without a place to go

In the lonely darkness –
No place for you to come
And yet
I know I must find strength
For both of us
To fly to where an island is,
Somewhere beyond
This awful night.

I will, I know I will,
But when the morning sun strikes down
Upon our feathers once again
Perhaps, and just perhaps
We'll find each other and some place to rest
Before the dark returns.

Souvenir

Do you remember how we came
That day to Huntsham Court,
Driving along through the maze of Devon lanes,
Narrow and steep, banks full
Of the summer flowers –
Foxgloves and scabious,
Cranesbill and mallow, and the cow parsley
Almost closing over the top of the car;
Innocent cottages moving in front of us,
Gardens ablaze, convolvulus
Plaited through their hedges;
And a dream of delphiniums,
Contrast of pale and dark,
Like our way through the months
Of our past most wonderful year?

It was a journey into an enchanted land,
I, still not entirely certain
If we should like the place
With its church lying in the hollow of the summer
wood;
You never questioning,
But both of us confirmed
In the joy of being together again.
Do you remember how it was?
You wore a white dress,
And it was such a lovely day,
With Friesian cows lying at the back of the hedges,

Opposite: Cabar feidh © Alasdair McMorrine

When we finally came to Huntsham Court,
Standing among the rough-cut grass,
And the parkland trees,
The whole of it somehow unreal
And suspended in time.
It was almost as though
An angel had made the place,
For there was the old, old house,
With never a soul in sight.

And the weeds on the gravel,
And the grey stone birds on the roof.
It was a lovely place, my One
A place we shall never forget,
The people who worked in the house,
German, American, Danish, Greek,
Seemed quite untouched by time.
There was a bluebottle inside our room –
You thought it was a bee –
And my shoes squeaked on the parquet floors.
But oh! The house was wonderfully cool
In the heat of the afternoon.
We were both rather tired,
But we loved each other with all of the rushing
wildness,
Bred from the absent days.

Afterward we slept in each other's arms,
As the evening slipped through the countryside.
There were two baths side by side in the bathroom
And a bidet that didn't work!
It was a lovely place.
Dinner was good,

There was music and no one else.
You sat, with your burnished hair,
And your smiling eyes,
And the glorious set of your mouth which I know
so well,
Framed by the two candles,
Listening to Rachmaninov,
Till the darkness dropped
Over the dreaming fields.

At night,
We slept, and when we woke in each other's arms
once more,
It was morning and time to leave
The wonderful place of our peace
In the green paradise.
We drove back to the world
Through the cobwebs of the wild flowers,
Do you remember?
With our thoughts of that ghostly place,
And the pledge of our hearts to each other,
Looking for honey that we never found.

And if,
If we are ever old, my One,
I shall always remember
That day we drove through the Devon lanes
To the place which you found,
Far, far away on the ultimate edge
Of reality.

For Ena Kendall, Journalist, Observer Magazine

Ena,
Do you remember how you came
Those many summer moons ago
And made me sit
Among the litter of my useless life?
You questioned me and then
The lights went out
At moments critical
For taking photographs
To illustrate your text,
But all the warmth
Of your humanity
Shone through the article that you wrote.
I feel so bad
I never thanked you properly
For so much trouble that you took.
Come back some day, some spring
When all the flowers are out again –
But bring your overcoat!

For Roger Ellis

I watched in the shadow
Of childhood days
Among remembered hills
When the wheels of your bicycles
Used to traverse the tracks
Under a forest of pines
The trees filled with crested tits.
Those were days when the air was alive
With a promise that's unfulfilled.
You have done better than I
For you've fitted your pupils for life
While I, not knowing which road to take
Have lost myself in a maze
With nothing to leave behind
But a torrent of wasted words.
I have fought quite hard for a very long time
And much enjoyed the fight
But now that the end is near
I look at the tireless hills
That man has sought to control
And looking, one suddenly knows
That the passage of one man's life
Is of terribly little importance
In the ultimate scheme of things.

Prickles

Oh! Prickles
You let me down –
You've turned the whole world upside down
First you were a girl,
Now you're a boy,
In those days when, the world
Turned clockwise
And the Earth revolved around the Sun
There wasn't the same
Uncertainty
The geese went home
Margaret was a girl
I was a boy
Snow fell in winter
And we ate strawberries
From the well strawed beds
Under the nets
Ripened in the endless summer sunshine days.

Rowan Berries Turning Red

Oh! What's the point
Of all the beauty of these Autumn days
With no one here to share
And hold my hand?

❧ ❧ ❧ ❧ ❧

Oh! What's the point
Of you not sitting here
Beside me in the evening in your chair
Listening to music as
The darkness slips along
The corridors of night?

❧ ❧ ❧ ❧ ❧

Life seems to have such little meaning
Without the beauty shared,
Either in silence or
With whispered words
Beside the teatime fire.

❧ ❧ ❧ ❧ ❧

I know you're there
Somewhere too far away to touch
But know so well your absent voice
Within my silenced ears.

❧ ❧ ❧ ❧ ❧

Know, too, my eyes which look for you,
With yours still gleaming,
But now, alas, striving in vain to see
As clearly as they used to do,

And needing me too often now
To translate into words

❧ ❧ ❧ ❧ ❧

All of the landscapes which we both
Have learnt through quite long lives
To watch, and love, and understand
As part of us, adding a meaning
To our every day.
Oh! What's the point
Without you there?

❧ ❧ ❧ ❧ ❧

And answer came there none!

Autumn, Loch Ossian © Alasdair McMorrine

Nedd and Ben

We live with some conceit
In 1, Irene Road,
Our coats are very sleek
And we know we are superior
To cats in other streets.

Our names are Nedd and Ben
Although the visitors are apt to call
Us ‘n’ cats, or, ‘chats’, or beasts,
We have a servant quite unlike
The cats along the street.

She feeds us coq au vin;
We dine at half past six;
For us no smelly mouse
Like cats in Parsons Green
In every other house.

We’re too well bred to work
Like cats in common roads
Who do not have a maid to serve,
Who pee upon the Persian rugs,
And slaughter little birds.

Because we do not pay
Our cleaner very much
A part time job to make her take
In order that she can afford
To have a little break.

We do not pay her stamp,
Pretend she's self-employed,
And on the whole we're happy that
She knows her place as servant
To these two conceited cats.

RUTH FROM MARYBURGH

She sits behind the desk
With her crown of dark hair
And her smiling voice –
Only a receptionist, she said –
Dealing out tea and justice
To the customers
At Radio Highland.

Early morning outside
In Culduthel Road
With the birds singing
In the quietness
As though there had never been
Spring before
In Inverness.

In the cool place
Which is a model
That other BBC offices
Should emulate
The victims about to be interviewed
Are calmed by the charm
Of Ruth
From Maryburgh.

Charles and Tugela at Garrogie

How can I give you thanks
For all the kindness that you showed me
The night you took me in at Garrogie,
Making me feel at home.
I took your salt, and lay in bed awake
Hearing the rutting stags
Roaring against each other
In the rising wind.
Outside the window panes
I heard the waters rushing down at dawn,
Watching the whiteness of the melting snow
As light crept up across the hills –
And then I went away
Filled with a hundred memories of both of you
Feeling that if the world was ever wrong
I'd found two friends who'd never let me down.
So thank you for that time of peace I found
Under your autumn roof
At Garrogie.

HEART'S EASE

Summer is slipping into September
Among these rainswept hills
With playing of a hundred martin's wings
Round and round outside my tower.
I sit alone with nothing but the thoughts
Of all that might have been
If God had cast his dice
Another way, but as it is
Can only listen to the whisper
Of the south west wind
Among the leaves of Tom Fool's chestnut tree
Outside my bedroom ledge
Where it has stood six centuries
Guarding the fords of Esk below
The granite Eskdale fells as they turn
From the longest to the shortest day.

All I can do is spin a dream
Hoping to lie again, just once, before I go,
Beside you in the heather
Among the blue hills, I love so much.

Mingled Hearts

I love the way we sleep at nights,
Laying our bones along each other's backs,
Guarding the sanctuary of our two mingled hearts,
That when, at times, we wake
We both are conscious of the two way facing fort
That keeps us safe.

And when we have to lie sometimes
Far far apart in other places,
The memory of how things are
Between the two of us
Is one more couple in the chain
That links us to our future hopefulness.

West Cumberland

A land of ancient stone
And ancient prejudice.
This is a place where Dane and Roman meet
Mixing their pedigrees;
Where Spanish ships were wrecked in 1588.
The strange invaders mingled
With the native race,
Proud, independent, slow to arouse,
Slow to appease.

This is forgotten territory, west of the Lakeland
fells,
Moulding each generation to the shape
And texture of their grim grey rocks.
Year after year men till the bitter land,
Cut trees, remove the stones to make the dykes,
And hew a meagre living from the hostile soil,
Tending the Herdwick sheep.

The people show great kindness,
But mists close in around them and their families;
Grey hills, grey rocks, grey skies
And in the kitchens men with wives to keep
Turn grey with worry at their overdraft,
Thinking about next spring.

For some no spring will come
Among those fields they know so well,
And when the hazel banks beside the becks
Turn fresh again with daffodils,
The hills will witness one more tragedy –
No cow to milk in the empty stall of the byre;
No orphan lambs in the boxes by the kitchen
stove;
A board at the end of the road –
"For Sale" it says.

WAITING FOR YOU

I'm working late tonight.
The wind has blown all day
Out of the west,
Tearing the clouds to tatters
On the noonday hills.
At three o'clock I drove along the road
That runs beside the sea.
I watched the sun
Lighting the maelstrom of the angry waves
I saw the foresters, stopped felling in the gale,
Clearing the rubbish where they'd thinned
The dark arcades of ancient oaks
Along the bottom drive.
The forage harvester
Was broken in the sudden silence of the silage
field,
The men were swearing at the fractured tines.
The only thing that seemed at peace
Were all the sheep
Who lay like Samuel Palmer paintings
In the sheltered fields.
So now it's night, and I am working late
Because it seems the quickest way to pass the
time
Until the hours between us finally vanish.
I wait for you.

GARETH'S FAREWELL

I've only gone away
Beyond some far-off hill
To find a place to wait for you.
You know we used to talk
About there not being an after-life,
But as you watch the arrowheads of geese
Pointing their way across the northern skies
You'll realise that we, perhaps,
Were not quite right.

My spirit has a cargo load
Of memories of you
For now I've learnt to know,
Though it be ages hence,
Our minds need never forget
To talk the way we always used to do.
So don't be lonely on your lonely journey
And learn to laugh again
Even if for a while we have to wait
For you to catch me up
Vaulting across the moonlit sky.

GOTHS AT THE GATES OF EDINBURGH
The threatened dispersal of
the Scottish National Portrait Gallery

Money and politics
Are kittle cattle when
The arts are being dismissed
By Thatcherite philosophies.
The truth is probably that Government
Dislikes the way
The council cleans the streets.
No politician dares to state it publicly,
But Glasgow city fathers have for years
And years administered their cash
With quite a lot of common sense,
While Edinburgh, our very heart,
Has sickened its inhabitants
With escalating costs.

I ask myself
Is that the reason why
It is proposed
Our well loved Scottish portraits should
Be now removed, after a hundred years,
From walls on which they rightfully belong,
Leaving our capital bereft
Of an inheritance it should not be
Allowed to be without!

Raeburn would turn inside his grave
To contemplate their base intentions now
But might permit his ghost a smile
On reading in *The Scotsman* of the boy
Who murmured 'aye' in Court and ended up
In jail. Let's hope
Raeburn may have the last laugh yet!

If not, I pray – God, how I pray –
His ghostly brushes may be mobilised
immediately
To paint graffiti on the empty walls!

Fallen Angels

I'm very tired,
And need a place to rest
Before we take the next great plunge
Across our lives.
The wind has blown incessantly
For days and days
Out of the west,
Driving the seabirds miles inland
And when I stand at night
Beside the old tower door,
Before the dogs are put to bed,
I hear the waves beat far away
Upon the sand
Beside the dunes at Drigg.

The wind
Has made me nervous now.
Often I watch the tattered moonlit clouds
Drive silently across the windowpanes,
But cannot sleep,
Waiting for minute hands to tick around the
clock
And mark the time that I come
To you.

I eat but little,
Try my best
To help the fallen angels strewn about
What seems my pointless path.
And so each day slides slowly on its way
Along the corridors of time,
As slowly, too, but certainly,
We pass across the absent hours,
Until we meet ourselves again.

At Carnan à Bhairrich © Alasdair McMorrine

SCOTLAND

We may never be rich
But let us at least
Strive to be wise
And kind.

This is our land
Which bred us the way that we are,
Obstinate –
Sometimes as hard as rocks,
Chiselled by years of wind;
Sometimes as soft as the murmur of spring
Through the branches of May-time trees.

Deep in our hearts,
Though some of us be
At four generations' remove
From our fathers' fields,
Scraping our living in faraway streets,
We have never forgotten
The land.

There are politicians,
Too far now from the soil,
Who ought to know better,
Who have totally failed
To understand –

continues...

And a government,
Unwilling to listen,
Careless of poverty,
Careless of people less well off
Than their handful of hard-faced men
Who work on the principle
Of plus or minus a few per cent;
Who hold a belief which is apt to ignore
Anything else but the short term gain.

Relief

From dawn today
I sat behind my desk,
Reading minutes, answering letters,
Paying the bills the weeks had brought,
At eight o'clock, the telephone –
Local, irrelevant.
The farmer had bought a bull!
At eight fifteen another call –
London enquiring if I'd signed
A contract for a book.
Again and again it rang.
The fox had eaten the builder's hens.
Did I know the Muscovy ducks were out?
Nothing to counteract the panic and the morning gloom
Until, at last, at half past eight,
The call I'd waited for –
Waited for all my life –
Your voice alight
With all the missing passion of the last six days.
I saw quite well the autumn sun
Outside the baker's shop from which you telephoned,
Knowing the world was good for us,
For you, the burning glory of my life,
Had put the universe to rights again.
How did I have so little faith
When fourteen nights ago last night
I slept within your arms?

One Moon More

I had no right
To place a single footstep
Through the door
That marked the threshold
Of your settling life

I had no right
To taste the warmth
That lay behind your smile
And call in mine
For those few glorious moments spun
From time.

Before you went away
I did not think
I could be moved sufficiently
To feel the touch
Of all the thoughts and humour
That you stained upon the darkness
Of my waiting night.

Perhaps I wronged you when I took
So much of all that generosity
You never hid
Behind your eyes,
Your half-expectant smile.

But now I feel so much the light
You flung about this place
And not the darkness
Of the night outside.
Meanwhile I wait for you
And your return.

For one moon more I'll wait,
Knowing one day
The Gods have written that we'll meet again
Beyond the silence of the hours
When you are gone.

Aberdona – for Brian and Lucy Poett

I have been happy in this place,
At ease with friends I hardly knew till now,
My last two weeks have been
Some of the most exhausting in my life.
Rushing from Skye to Edinburgh,
From Ayr to Aberdeen,
London and back to Muncaster,
Dreading each time I've had to speak
At meetings
All of which needed original thought
To coax the clients to laughter
Or tears.

For a week I was ill,
So when I came here last night
Out of that grey and rainswept night
I felt quite utterly drained inside,
Almost too tired to think –
But your house is a miracle place,
Full of the two of you
And the home that you've made,
With the thought of the children's chatter
Combing the stillness of vacant rooms,
Handing me back my peace.

I shall never forget the time I spent
Under your sheltering roof
With all the kindness you gave
To an almost stranger,
And the thought of children's voices
Soon to return to a house
At perfect peace with itself.

Afterwards

Oh! High hills of my heart,
Harbour my soul to its dock
Among the grey rocks
And the merciless winds.
Lay down my weariness in the mantles
Of your fresh snow and let me sleep.
Oh! Let me sleep.

Lay my head on the stones of your high tops
Beside the ptarmigan on Aonach Beag
Or the Binnein Shuas above Loch na h-Earba,
Where I lay one glorious day
In the warmth of the July sun
A month of summers ago.

Rally my failing strength
To soar with the wings of the eagle
Over the corries where I harried the wild deer
Without mercy in the days of my youth.
Rally my dreams awhile
Then give me sleep!
Now the deer are safe
The hinds and the dappled calves
Curled in the heather clumps,
And the stags away from the flies
On the high tops until September time.

Later, much later, with the rising of the resin
The melting snow will cleanse the wounded
heart
In the clouded burns above
Where they rush underneath the rowans
In the cracks of rock, down to the Spean
Till then, just let me sleep.
With my soul free to roam
Over the grey moss and the slopes
Which were my home
In times before.

Thank you, Oh!, thank you
High hills of my heart,
For all that you have been – and are.
Please take me soon,
Please take me home
And let me sleep!
People will say, 'he's dead',
But then it will be spring
And time of dream-come-true
At last.

I Met a Robin

Beloved One,
You sleep tonight outside my arms,
With miles and miles of France
Between us both.
The days troop sadly by
With you not here,
Their dull recession broken only
By the violent storms.
The land is tired this week,
And trees lie down to die,
And gold medallions fill the stormy days,
Where leaves give their late pretence
Of summer dance
And wander aimlessly about the autumn sky.

I met a robin in the hall one day,
The greylags seek the sheltered pools,
While in the wind-tossed woods
The fallen trees,
Roots weakened by the summer drought,
Release their hold upon the sodden soil.
It is a time of tears,
With ancient friends cast motionless upon the
ground.

I ask myself, 'Will spring return,
Will you?'
This week it rained
As though the Gods were cross,
But when you telephoned
The sun came out
And all the world was pacified –
Including me,
For then I knew once more
That all my world
Included you!

DEAREST ALBYN*

I picked the first camellias
In the Church Wood
In November this year
At Muncaster,
But my heart is elsewhere,
And not in what I have to do here.
People are kind to me in this place,
Which is very beautiful,
But I miss the hills and the skies
Of my own land –
So much.

Please be kind to me, too,
Because for me
You are Scotland,
And I know, from our very brief meetings,
Even so early in our knowledge of each other,
That if I drop in the battle,
It is you who will pick up the standard,
And be in the front
Of the fight.

My heart is yours
Always within you,
Wherever you make
Your home
Your stand.
If I can give nothing else,
At least I can give you this,
Knowing my country is utterly safe
In your hands.

Birches © Alasdair McMorrine

LORD HAVE MERCY UPON US!

'Small farmers,'
The County Secretary said,
(They call him Ward in case you didn't know!)
'They'd like to hear from you,'
That's me he meant – the optimistic chap!
Well thou'd best look in t'mirror of thy brand new
Volvo,
If thou think'st anything I may say might be
applied to thee.

Do not let anyone in Cumberland – or
Westmorland,
(Can't be doin' w' t' mongrel names they give us
now!)
Say we aren't well represented – NFU I mean.
If anyone tells me Joe Raine don't fight
Quite hard enough for us,
I'll punch his nose.

(Bit strong, mebbe, for all the toffs from east the
hills!)
Like Michael Jopling, I can't understand,
The dairy industry:
Don't read the *Farming News*, and rather deaf,
So not quite certain I have heard,
The people in the market talking reet,
But likely Quayle, he understands,
And Allison's a crafty bloke.

Willie Rawling drummed off t'Planning Board,
It really was a damned disgrace,
For he knew what the county needed.
Small farms the only way,
To populate the countryside.
As I should know for I've four daughters
As wild as Herdwick yowes!
Small farms go – no one left to pay the rates,
Or pick up litter for they Conservation folk.
Twelve bore gun is no deterrent
Over fifty yards,
So what's t'use o' greet big fields
When they don't shut the gates!
Actually most of them is queet a'reet!

Small farmer backbone of the countryside,
So Butler said! Boss of the NFU
Let's have some action and a little less
O' eloquence from Agriculture House,
And Gourlay wi' his lofty views,
And all that lot.

Please!

Big farmer makes small farmer go,
'Reducing overheads' he said,
But then big farmer's dead
(A coronary, I think!)
For did you see his latest statement,
From the local Nat. West. Bank,
(A little advert as they're good to me sometimes!)
It's all – and very – like the sunset,
Red.

Big o/d means need for higher prices;
Farmer can't afford to take less,
Then consumer doesn't like it!
And nor does Her in Downing Street
The Governess, I mean!
Small farmer driven out and can't afford,
To live in t'countryside,
So goes to town, nothing to do.
It isn't an efficient way to use a countryside, y'know
Particularly in West Cumberland,
Where small farms always ruled OK.

Now even our Co-operative which started here
Is gettin' high and mighty for the most o' us,
And talks about the need for only ten tonne loads.
Struth! They'll need wings to tak' them in,
To some o' they West Cumbrian steadings.
Tractors rather good, but much too dear
For most small farms.

It's people – lots of them – we need in t'countryside,
Not things!
(By people I mean persons wi' a mind that's all
their own,
And that means Herdwick yowe in t'cabbage patch
Is still a'reet!)

I ken quite weel
What Governments are used to thinking.
For we're like her (t'Herdwick yowe, I mean!)
A lot of complicated awkward folk –
But here we stay!

So just give o'er Jopling lad,
And find a scheme which keeps us quiet,
Or we will surely twist,
Your servile politician's tail,
When Doomsday comes
In 1988.
And then She'll have to hoick you up,
And find a place in t'other House.

We need a rural policy,
That says enough's enough.
We need small farms as social assets.
We need commitment from our representatives.
So come on lad you've left it rather late.

My wildest daughter's had to emigrate!

Magic Words

My shining star,
You hid your head these two weeks past
Behind the clouds that hang about the mountain tops.
Without your light
I fancied for a while
That I was lost
Among the labyrinthine paths of life.

But now,
The sombre clouds
Are lifting from the far hillsides
And once again I hear your dear beloved voice,
Can almost touch your face
Across my desk.
You came to me last night at sleeping time,
And told me one day soon
You'd hold my hand,
And lead me out from all the awful blackness
That your absence brought
To this, my dark, dark land.

Of course it's wrong,
Wrong to rely on stars to steer one home,
When stars may hide in clouds
Above the equinoctial seas.

But you, my shining star,
Eclipse them all,
The clouds, the foaming waves,
The showers of falling autumn leaves that have
begun to fall
Upon the sodden lawns.

And soon
I hope you'll hear the magic words
Along the distant wires
'You're welcome home'

Another Message from the Hills

We have been lucky
Who have learnt
Through years and years
Of culling deer and herding sheep
The magic of the Highland hills;
Hearing the wind on winter nights
Driving the snow in drifts
Across the barren lands
And in beneath the doors of byres
Or through the dark arcades of pines.
Often we've watched the moon
Shed light across the loch
Going to far off meetings
An hour before the dawn.
We've learnt a consciousness
Of all that went before
And tried to use it for the benefit
Of those who needed homes and jobs –
And yet, go out
Into the streets of Inverness,
You won't walk far
Before you find a man who says,
'Landowners are privileged parasites
Who rape our land;
Control the lives of
Whole communities
For whom they do not care one jot;
Seek to exclude
The people from the hills;
Plant trees to spoil the scenery;

Puncture the mountain bikes
By leaving stones about the land
Bully the government for private gain.'
Some of you I have known
Since childhood days.
Fathers of others I served beside
During my National Service
In the Camerons.
Some of you have, from time to time
Annoyed me quite immoderately:
Those who too often come
Out of necessity from far away,
Arrive exhausted from their city desks,
Contributing little enough
To life in the communities
In which they live
A bare eight weeks a year.
Too often they don't understand
The deep resentment of
The native populace
Who sometimes hide their thoughts
Behind their Highland courtesy.
I try to represent you
In the fairest light I can
Through all of this and that,
But God! It's sometimes difficult.
I hope you understand the reason
That I cannot say I'll guard you
When you break the law.

The job of your Convenor
Is to talk to politicians,
Often a little ignorant,
Quite hostile to the private
Ownership of land;
Led by the nose by conservationists
Who hardly ever have
To make a living from the soil,
Coming from cities miles away.
He has to talk to civil servants
And the Press;
To all of them, on your behalf,
He has to try to put a smile
Of innocence and goodness
On his face,
Even though the thoughts of
Some of you
Are sinister.
Of all of you
I do not always totally approve.
I know quite well, at worst
You sometimes don't approve of me.
At best, you merely think me mad.
And yet, you know that
When I speak
I try to speak the truth
For you – and when I say for you,
I also mean the Scottish land.
To serve you is the greatest honour
I could have.

Our times are difficult.
Our houses cost a lot to keep.
Our land still needs the care
It always needed.
But now the things it can produce
Cannot maintain the past
The way the past demands.
My forecast is
On some tomorrow we shall see
A parliament in Edinburgh
A government in London,
Just as now,
For which we do not care,
For which we have a mutual respect;
With vicious councils here
And there,
Peopled by men whose fathers were
Treated quite badly
By an absent laird –
And on that day remember me
Because my job is now
To talk to everyone,
Trying to persuade them all,
Owning the land we own,
We have a part to play,
Not in the past,
But in tomorrow;
Not just upon our own behalf
But for the people

Who depend on us.
Too often now land has become
No more than a commodity
To buy or sell,
But you know, and I hope
Our children know
The land needs love.
We do not own the land,
The land owns us,
But while I live
I'll fight my best for you
To prevent
The constant whittling
Of your rights
Which all the time is limiting
The contribution
That we can and ought
To make.

Left, Eilean na Righ © Alasdair McMorrine

MESSAGE TO LORD SANDERSON

Scotland has had enough
Of all the verbal massacre
Of party politics today
Those of us who once believed,
Cannot believe in the austerity.
The stark simplicity,
The Government preach at us
About the economics of the market place.
There had to be a change of medicine
From government in 1979
But oh! My God, we had it
Handed out as by an army matron
Dosing troops. Now
Her brave young acolytes
Are limbering up for office,
But now the cure has almost killed the patient.
Too much damage done.
The economic references were quite correct,
But <u>not</u> the style.
Style is important in democracy,
Survival vital for a business man.
If Tory principles are to retain some credibility
They do not need
A kamikaze pilot in the seat,
With whom the purity
Of party doctrine will finally put out
The guttering candle that some of us
Once held with so much hope

Is this to be the fate of Scotland
And her people?
Some saw we are ungovernable
I tell you quite, quite soon
If you should take this way
We'll prove we are!
Government must be seen and heard
To mind about the people,
For many of us now
Forsyth as Scottish Secretary
Would be the final blow,
'Out, out brief candle!'
Macbeth was right and we
Have had enough!
We badly need a spell
Of common sense!

Patrick of the Hills

My life is turbulent – and lonely
Chained to my desk
And reams and reams of useless paper
I sat last night among a group
Of ancient Cumbrian faces
Some by work, some by adoption
A most unlikely audience
In the theatre designed years by Oliver Messel
Listening to Beethoven
Beautifully interpreted by the Belcea Quartet
Surely four of the world's
Finest young musicians
And as the notes filled the theatre
I listened for us both
Reaching a hand across the night
Trying our fingers to touch
Across the storm outside,
So that this music might embrace
And make us one and pacify the storm
Until we set our sails
On calmer seas
Patrick of the Hills
I scuttle past the telephone
And try with difficulty not to do
What you told me not to do!

Land Reform

I say to the crofters
You have a future.
But do not listen to the twang
Of Jim Hunter's seductive harp
Or sermons by John Bryden
And Andy Wightman on land reform.
They preach with the words of reason
Because they have learnt how to trust them
But their theme is a past
Which never existed –
A tyrannic memory that has enslaved you.

Injustice there was,
But your predecessors went away from the land
For reasons of economics
Just as much as for avarice
Of greedy lairds.
Despite the legends of the past two hundred years
The land could not support them,
And cannot support them now,
Without the unsustainable use
Of subsidy from an urban purse
Entertaining what we all see
In the countryside
As a lifestyle equally unsustainable,
Which meets poverty on its daily doorstep
And quite often closes an eye.

continues...

It is they who are vast and democratic majority
So start building again yourselves,
Stone by stone, for a future
Which can last and adjust to change,
I, too, am a romantic, but plug your ears
To the lilt of the words
To which you have become so accustomed.
Learn a new song which will
Stand your children in better stead
And save them from the seduction
Of poets and preachers
With their own political agenda.
They are dangerous men.

An urban democracy
Is every bit as unkind
As a wicked laird from the past,
Both of them striving at the centre of power
To maintain the lifestyle
They have learnt to expect.

Crofting must continue
But do not trust the paymaster
Who can turn the financial tap to 'off'
Quicker than any plumber
In Balallan, Lochmaddy, or Portree.

I'M ALWAYS THERE

Looked mildly horrified
And nearly had a fit!

We had a ploughman's lunch
At the Bull, and admired the magnolia blooms
And roses on the houses beside the river.
We walked back to the car,
Your arm in mine,
God, how I love you whoever you are!

Then there was Kew,
And shades of the old botanists,
And the thought of their quartering the world
Searching for plants.
We went into a greenhouse Decimus
Burton had built in 1861.
(Almost as odd a name as Indiana Jones,
Didn't we think?)
Multi-coloured children everywhere,
And 'economic' plants,
Whatever, they may be!

Outside the yuccas were in flower.
And outside too, the wind in all the trees.
It seems that there must always be
Wind in the trees,
Sighing for you and me.

continues...

We went to the Maids of Honour
And had some tea.
It took eternity.
You dropped me at the Underground.
We kissed goodbye at Gloucester Road.

It hurts me that I cannot give
The one thing that you really need –
A place to rest,
To call your own.

I cannot give you ease
Or peace of mind,
Or somewhere quiet to lay your head at night,
I can give none of these.

I know you're frightened if I put a foot
Within the circle of the little limbo which
You made yourself;
Frightened
That you will give too much,
And take too much
That might be torn away.
Breaching your circle's frail security.

All I can do
Is wait in patience in the wings,
Saying a little prayer from time to time,
And stay still long enough to let you know
You're not alone.
I'm always there.

County Chairman

A loner, I,
Loathe every minute of
The pestilential meetings which
I have to referee.
I like the people, but
I set and feel
Like some poor butterfly
Impaled upon a pin –
Tied down by standing orders;
Constitutions; secretaries;
What can and can't be done;
And years and years of seasoned men
Who dot the 'i's,
And cross the 't's,
And like committees on
Which they have sat
Since time began,
They all enjoy the little points
They try to score
At my expense.

Meantime, the enemy,
The faceless ones in government offices,
Slip off the hook.
Committees bore me but,
Unlike the enemy,
Impaled
I can't escape.

continues...

The men we represent
Work patiently at home among the fells;
At nights, sometimes,
They voice opinions in the pub
Which do not always coincide
With what their representatives present
They may not understand
The finer points of logic which
The bureaucrats dream up,
But they, who make their living from the land
Are those we ought to think about –
Are those with problems
Which we need to solve.

Of course, we need them both,
The good committee men
And those who stay at home,
Although I often wonder if
They both need me.
And **that** is why
I loathe each minute of
The penitential meetings which
I have to referee.

I fear
Until my dying day,
A loner I
Shall always be!

By the Mountain Burns

I can't reach you today.
Can't see your face,
Nor hear the lilt of your dear voice,
Even down the distant telephone wires.

So now
I suppose I shall never wake
Up in your arms
And hear the robin sing
Songs under our bedroom window;

Never –
Fall asleep beside you
At peace
In our own bed,
Listening to the wind
And the tide running in the Island sounds.

Never –
Walk in the hills,
And sky the deer,
And hear the foxes call:
See snowdrifts pile
Against the forest fence.

continues...

Nor lie together by the mountain burns
Watching the trout
Flicking their tails
Among grey stones
In crystal pools.

For all that ‘Thou art my waking,
Thou my dreaming’,
For ever and always,
In this distant place of exile
So far from the home hills.

The garden is dead this morning
Without no birds singing
Here at Muncaster.
I am a prisoner of conscience,
And you are gone!

The Song of the Owl © Alasdair McMorrine

The Old Witch of Balbirnie – Doctor on a Hockey Stick

Jean Balfour of Balbirnie

(A fantasy for Elspeth Fraser's birthday)

I asked for a birthday card
In the delicatessen at North Bewick –
Of all places –
And the computer up with this:-
'Doctor on a Hockey Stick –
Not Dickson
Old witch – repeat question –
Dickson's daughter – young mother –
Many happy returns!'

If I were a little less scrupulous
I might stoop down quite low –
Magic methods, I mean –
And hire one of Tyrell's Tarts to do her up –
Two swift blows on the knee
With well aimed hockey stick,
Delivered with maximum precision,
Minimum force,
You see, I know the right people
To do the job!

As it is the Captain's mother's birthday
I'll satisfy my better mannered self
With drinking an infusion of her herbal tea
And reading leaves in the bottom of the cup
To weave a protection racket
Against the Old Witch of Balbirnie's spells
As she swoops through the skies at night

Over the roofs of Aberdour,
Her skirts on fire with Wee Willie's latest match
Before his E levels
Are finally reduced

It should work,
And I shall think of the Captain's
Father's begonias,
Slow to braird this year,
Winning first prize at the show again;
And her mother, whose birthday it is,
Listening with lighter heart
To the disappearing echoes
Until only a repetitive whisper remains –
'National Parks, National Parks
Will no one listen to my calls?
I'm cunning with Government.
I know best,
There's money in it, but nobody understands.
(Repeating Roger Carr!)
No one has any Scottish Pride!'

When you get this
I shall have eaten the last piece
Of my toast at breakfast time,
Before the Captain's Mother (capital M today)
Catches the London train;
And father goes to the Office:
And I, imitating the Fleet Air Arm,
Fly off in pursuit
Of the Witch!

A Letter

Darling,
Your letter came when I returned
To Muncaster.
I dared not climb the spiral stairs –
Afraid to open doors in case
The magic which we made
Escaped for good.
Your spirit hangs around me now,
Sitting in my office,
Writing to you.
I see so well your dear, dear eyes
Upon me as we drove
Those countless miles
Through hills and skies,
Each magic day unlimited;
Our life so short –
Like butterflies.

I feel your fingers' touch
Stretched out between the seats
To touch my arm:
Know now, no less than then,
The sheer delight
That night
We felt so strong
We had to celebrate –
A sort of coming home
For each of us, no one
Had warned us of, no one
Can ever imitate.

The music that we made
We made for Us,
For Us alone,
Just you and me,
Learning to lose ourselves
In something greater than us both,
Hearing the waves of Island seas
Among the caves,
And eagles' wings sweeping across the wind
At dawn
Above the mountain tops.

Darling, that is
Just how it was.
I can give you nothing, I know.
But everywhere I go
I find you waiting now –
On the road to Bangor,
Looking across the Menai Straits:
In my room at the Sychnant Pass
Where your roses came, charged
With all the passion that you said
You could not give
At Crewe.

In London where we've never walked,
I strolled on pavements through the wide arcades
Of cherry trees,
Shedding pink petals on the evening breeze

continues...

I watched the moor
Come up above the town
From Jameson Street
And turned my ten pence piece
For you, and still had ten pence more
To telephone.

I am
A bad man, that I know,
Can never come, I think,
To give you happiness for good
But please keep talking, all the same
My too late love.

Perhaps God, in his wisdom, may repent
And some day find a way.
If not,
What lay between us through the night
Of our short quite – togetherness
No god,
Not even He,
Can take away.

Teach Me To Be Wise

I don't want anything
That's second hand or second best for you
I never can give all of me
And my completeness
In the way I'd like to give,
But still I want to draw for you
The thoughts I think, the sights I see
When leaves are blowing through autumn skies
As some reflection of the joys I find
In giving you this much of me
That does not take away
From he someone else.

To me you are the crispness
And the cleanliness I taste
In eating apples when October comes.
I love you, I suppose,
From our brief knowing.
Teach me to give you,
If not quite completeness,
Then, at least,
The very best of some of me.

On Appointment as Vice-Convenor, SLF

I've much too much to do
But thought I'd let you know
And all the others in your offices
That because of you
Who do so much for me
How could I say
I would not help a year or two
And so my friends, I'll try to represent
The tribes that have not changed in centuries
Beneath their skins, except that now
They're forced to paint their sheep with woad
Instead of using it themselves
Being made to have a bath with soap
At night by English wives who call it
Civilised, although beneath
They're still inclined to fight with government
And you will have an awful job
To sop your latest Vice-Convenor
Joining in!

UNENDING HAPPINESS,,,

I am so frightened now
I've travelled much too far,
Too long without a rest to contemplate,
Tonight I feel ill –
Sore head, sore chest
And a bad tooth –
And the terror of life alone
Is very real.

Soon you will go to America
And you will say, quite rightly,
I can do nothing about the situation
But I begin to wonder if
I am not expected to make
All the sacrifices
Run the risks
So that now unjustly
In my mind I accuse you
For the feeling
Of my unwantedness.

I suppose I'm tired
And need a rest,
But without you now
After these past many years
Everything I believe in
Would soon be dead
If I ever need a confirmation

continues...

Of my need of you
This is it
Like the Afghan I watched
On the television today,
High above the road to Jallalabadm
I need a cause
And my cause must always be
Your unending happiness!

Horse Whisperer

We watched the old stallion, born
Not yesterday, among the mares we trailed
Under the branches of the Altyre woods
Then, finding each other's eyes
We recognized that similarity
Of you, unbroken yet,
Not able to endure the saddle's discipline,
The bridle's curb and I
Reaching the limits of an old
Invincibility,
No longer strong enough
To need a bit on my desires
To straddle your wildness and explore
The tension of your untamed limbs.

A Veterinary Dinner

The nearest I have ever come
To surgery would be
Too insignificant for you.
Early morning in the Scottish hills,
In circumstances quite insanitary
Replaced the calf bed of a cow too full;
Performing two caesarians
On two reluctant ewes,
The lambs lived, the ewes died,
Probably of septicaemia,
Leaving their progeny
As my eventual debt.
The cow survived, but I
Had learnt enough to know
It's best to leave the surgery
To you, and hope you make enough
To keep your wives equipped in luxury
With all the war paint
In a way they think
That is their due.

Mountain Sky

This time tomorrow I shall stand
among the mountain skies,
And lay my fingers on the wet unchanging rocks,
And let the peace seep down around my mind;
The self-deceptions of the year will ease away
Into the swirling greyness of the glens,
Just as the red deer glide along the ridge,
Fleeing the stalker's curses and his stinking scent,
Leaving the rattled stones as evidence
Upon the shrouded air
The truth remains.

This time tomorrow I shall stand
Among the echoes of the grieving burns
Shall hear the slack wind whisper in the pines
below,
And face the truth it whispered
When our magnet souls first met,
Those countless, countless moons ago.

Doubt not, mo chridhe, doubt not!
For when I stand among the weeping skies
The truth will be the selfsame truth I told you then
'I love you, not tonight, not yesterday,
But all night long and every day,
Beyond the very spans of time.'

Bernard Gooch Award

So here I stand in front of you
Honoured with a bowl too good
To crack across the heads
Of all the people who deserve a broken skull.
I have identified them, one by one,
Across the years I've been in Cumbria.
The Minister in charge of Sellafield who's undecided;
The architects of structure plans which state
The west coast is for quiet enjoyment, nothing more;
The Highway Authority with its idiotic definition of
'Not dangerous' or 'difficult' at Ambleside;
The dreadful perpetrator of the ugly bridge
Across the Esk at Muncaster;
Director of the CTB who wouldn't live in Cumbria.
People whose policies have done no service to
The home my wife has had to keep.

But I, I do not deserve a beautiful bowl
For all I've done is what you all would do,
Faced at the age of fifty-two
With deficits of £50,000 a year notched up by
someone else;
Armed with a house and garden that my wife
Persuaded me – and her – to keep,
Full of dry rot and leaking roofs.
Competing with a thousand such like homes
We lived in genteel poverty beside a freezing fire
And gave the natives quite a douche of character,
Keeping buckets underneath the holes through which
We watched the weeping sky.

I didn't always like the CTB. Time was
Directors seemed to change no less than once a year,
And though the number of the telephone
Was easy to dial by memory
It never was exactly like hitting the jackpot at
The end of Blackpool Pier.

It really was no use our home being just another house,
Losing serious money with the parrots and the bears.
We've had to be outrageous, with dogs in residence,
Sitting in priceless chairs.
The public seemed to like it. Bit by bit
We sacked the bank as creditor
And learnt to like the visitors a lot.
We got demands to speak at public meetings
And learnt to detest words by which we had to live –
Tourism and English Heritage.

We live like pigs, but Muncaster again
Exists to serve the people of West Cumbria,
And now its time for nimbler brains and younger heads
To steer the ship across the rocks,
But whatever the future holds
I shall always remember the kindness
Of all the people who have helped us –
Our guides and gardeners, cleaners and building staff
The farmers in the fells, the TICs, the Tourist Board
And all of you; and if you forget me as sure as fate
I shall be back as one more bona fide ghost
At Muncaster.

continues...

The house will continue as a family home.
The value of history is not in its past
But in the lessons we can learn from it.
Today you've honoured me
Far and away beyond my just deserts.
Tonight I must be a hundred and fifty miles away,
Yet wherever I am, for the rest of my life,
I pledge myself to your service –
And to the service of all the people
Of Cumbria.

Illness

Life for me is only about one thing
Now that we have passed the meridian
It's about you.
Some days when I am ill like this,
Finding it hard to breathe,
The miles between us seem impassable –
Can't telephone,
Don't want to eat,
And sleep is only a merciful interlude
Before the return of the awful aches
Your absence spells.
Outside my bedroom windows skies rush by
With rain and mist incessantly.
At three o'clock it's almost dark.
The tides are high. The valley floods.
Meantime, I live another week,
Soon it will be
Another year – and then, perhaps,
Time of more hope
And less impossibility.

In Perfect Time

Three years is quite a lot
Of time to pass
Beneath the bridge
That links the valley farms.
Three years ago today
You came from nowhere into my life
Unexpected, not awaited,
Unsummoned
Quite uncalculated
Do you remember?
Since then you've never been
One single moment out of mind
So intimate
Our limbs seem one,
Our thoughts
In perfect time.

That day you came
I heard a wind
Run rustling through the summer trees
And found your mental hand
Reached out to mine,
Our minds at one,
Knowing unconsciously
Each others needs.
Do you remember?

Since then we've walked and run
A mile or two,
In fits and starts.
You've been across the world and back
A time or two
As I have seen America.

But now I'm sick of distant love
And need you home
Beside me in the night
To listen to the wind
That changes tune with age
And tells us time apart
Spells waste.

I Miss You

I'm very lonely now without you there
Beside me in the night.
I miss a home, a room, a bed;
I don't want anybody else,
But only you;
And now having discovered you at last,
After so long,
I feel deprived,
Knowing that though our arms are stretched out,
Only when we are close
Might there be rest.

You see, I know
You are, of course, quite close
All of the time,
But now I miss so much
The sheer joy of sleeping
Within the circle of your arms,
With you in mine,
Hovered between happy dream and wakefulness
And where,
In that so strange and unexpected countryside
We found each other, and an utter happiness.
And that is why,
Although I know that I no longer am alone,
I feel so lonely here tonight,
Without you by my side.

At Newlands End

For Ann and David Curry

How could it take until now
All of my sixty years
To find my way to this place
To the home of my late met friends
That I hardly knew before
Yet feel I have known quite well
For the whole of my reckless life.

As I sit in the window writing
In the room at the top of the stairs
Watching the dawn's grey stealth
Slipping through spring green fields
The birds are starting to sing
In the new leaf trees outside
And grey dawn doves are calling,
And a plump cock pheasant struts
At the end of the well kept garden
Where malevolent winds are rising
Bending the willows at will
Prelude to violent storm.

It feels like a home should feel,
At one with its peaceful self.
I have met a great many people
But why did I have to wait
For the whole of a dissolute life
To find you all in this place
At one in your clockwise world?

continues...

Why has it taken so long
To hear of your childrens' hopes;
To take the salt at your table,
Only spoilt by the unfilled place
Of the father who came and went
Through the hours of the passing night
Without having time to speak
To his drills of awaiting shallots.

I don't suppose that you know
You are holding something fine,
Less fickle than party games
Fought by political cats –
More precious than any gold,
Something that very few have
Something you must not lose,
However long you may live.

Soon I shall have to go,
But the sight you gave to a friend
Will give him new vigour again
For another round of the fight,
And endless regret at the wasted years
Of not having known you before
Or your charm of delightful daughters
Who could twiddle me round their thumbs –
But I am rapidly reaching the end
So thank God
I can't turn my clock back
To being twenty years old again.

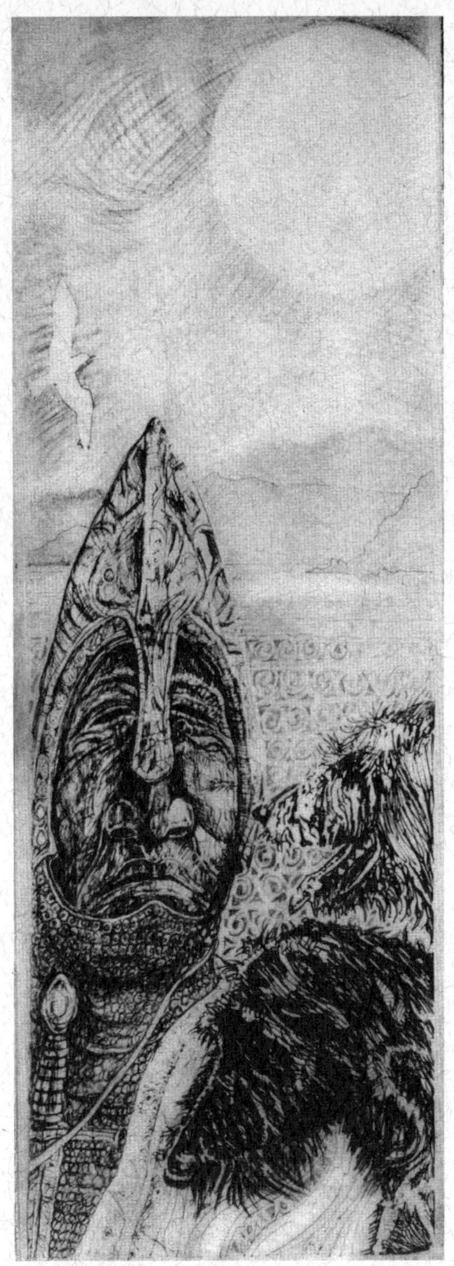

The Black Dog's Day has not yet come

Notes on the Illustrations

Beyond Creag Uanach (page 12)

Reflections Loch Laggan (page 23)

Cabar Feidh (page 37 the Stag's Antlers)
One of the most popular and lilting tunes, which was often requested by Highland regiments when marching. Included in the print are images that combine reality, legend and the harsh and hugely devastating effects of two World Wars. A poignant group of survivors from the 1915 Battle of Loos is juxtaposed against a chaotic foreground that blends Pictish carvings, the antlered Celtic god Cernunnos and creatures from the Apocalypse. The grave slab at the top of the print is based on the Oransay Stones which were produced during the late flowering, in the sixteenth century, of the West Highland Carving Schools. It also makes reference to the proud Mackenzie motto of 'Cuidich 'n Righ' (Defend the King). It is said that one of their archers saved King Alexander III from being gored by a wounded stag and that he then gave their clan the right to use this motto.

Autumn Loch Ossian (page 45)

Carnan a' Bharraich (page 60 at the grave of the Barra-men)
Colonsay and Oransay, at the outermost edge of the Inner Hebrides, have provided a richness of archaeological finds dating from the earliest Mesolithic sites to Bronze Age forts and Viking burials. Every age has left its traces upon the landscape. The grave of the Barra-men, excavated by Symington Grieve in 1913, revealed the strakes and rivets of a longship together with armour and grave goods that

used both Pagan and Christian symbols. Many of these symbols display a delightful 'hedging of bets' in that they leave the doors open to both Heaven and Valhalla. This would have been a sensible protection for the descendants of both Keitel Flat Nose and Godred the Black.

Birches (page 73)

Eilean an Righ (page 84 the King's Island)
Loch Laggan has been favoured since ancient times as a hunting site of great beauty and importance. There are chambered tombs at Ardverikie, a Bronze Age fort at Dun da Lamh and Cille Choinneich, a Columban site, at Kinlochlaggan. According to local legends Pictish kings hunted in the Laggan area. It is said that they were converted to Christianity and that they were buried on Eilean an Righ with their faithful hunting dogs being laid to rest on nearby Eilean nan Con. Both sites may have been crannogs.

The print was inspired by the carvings on Pictish stones that bring that important Early Medieval era so vividly to life. The Pictish rulers of the ninth century used symbols to both decorate their tombs and cross slabs and to inform their subjects. These symbols were produced by a sophisticated and creative society. The craftsmen used bold and animated naturalism to portray the Picts as being wise, religious and powerful. In the print King Fergus, like the biblical King David, plays his harp to soothe and protect his people. The snake, the salmon or ferox, the stag and the startled osprey all suggest knowledge, strength vision and leadership in times of invasion and uncertainty.

Oran na Comhachaig (page 97 the Song of the Owl)
The print is inspired by this epic poem, which was composed on Loch Treigside by the Keppoch bard Donald son of Finlay of the Songs. The main themes are revealed through his dialogue with an owl who foretells the rise

and fall of the clan. There is praise of the hunting on Creag Uanach and of the Keppoch chiefs. There are laments for the leaving of well-loved places and for the coming of old age:

> *From my hilltop I look with longing on Creag Uanach, sunshine bathed, and my thoughts turn to the bustle of the hunt, the eagle's scream from on high, the call of the cuckoo, the cry of the swan – these were my company.*

Thig latha a' choin duibh fhathast (cover and page 119, the Black Dog's Day has not yet come)
The Colonsay chieftain Murdoch MacFie owned the most beautiful black hound that seemed more content to laze in front of the fire than to exercise or hunt. His guests used to tell him to kill the Black Dog as it was not worth feeding. MacFie would reply 'Let the beast alone, its own day is still to come.' In a marvellous blending of folk lore and historical tradition the dog dies defending his master. Some versions of the tale have the murderers as clan raiders while others have them as supernatural creatures. The seagull in the print refers to the death, a century later, of Malcolm, the last MacFie chief. Whilst hiding from his MacDonald enemies in a sea pool on Eilan nan Ron his presence was betrayed by screeching seagulls. He was captured an executed.

For more information: http://andrewmcmorrine.com

Read More

books by Patrick Gordon-Duff-Pennington

Patrick of the Hills, Arena Press

Last Post and Reveille, 978-1-904524-96-0

Those Blue Remembered Hills, 978-1-910237-10-6

You can buy these books by visiting Muncaster Castle
or your local bookshop.

www.muncaster.co.uk